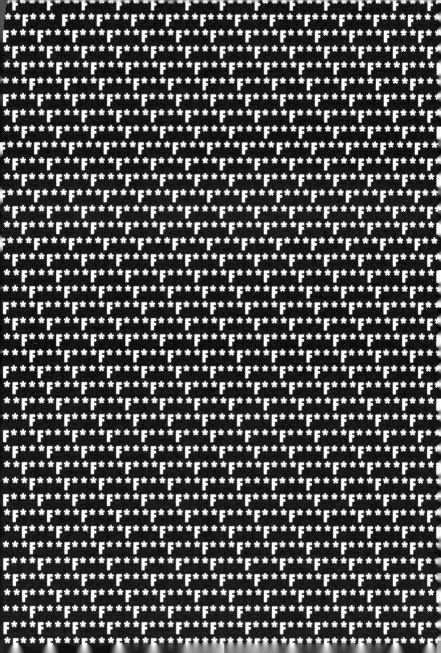

BREXIT:
JOIN THE
F***ING DOTS

JAMIE WHYTE

DEDICATED TO:

Alice, for staying strong and stable
Lucy, for securing a deal
And Helen, for remaining

BREXIT:
JOIN THE
F***ING DOTS

An Hachette UK Company
www.hachette.co.uk

First published in Great Britain in 2018 by Pyramid,
an imprint of Octopus Publishing Group Ltd
Carmelite House, 50 Victoria Embankment, London EC4Y 0DZ
www.octopusbooks.co.uk

ISBN 978-0-7537-3335-6

A CIP catalogue record for this book is available from the British Library

Printed and bound in China

10 9 8 7 6 5 4 3 2 1

Publisher: Lucy Pessell
Designer: Lisa Layton
Editor: Sarah Vaughan
Production Controller: Katie Jarvis

HERE ARE THE ARCHITECTS AND CHEERLEADERS OF BREXIT IN THEIR OWN WORDS

All the dotty, honestly-they-really-said-that things they said are written out right next to their dotty faces, just so it's really f***ing clear when you are trying to connect the dots and make sense of the bigger picture here.

YOU WANT TO KNOW HOW THIS HAPPENED? JOIN THE F***ING DOTS.

"This idea that what people want is an in-out referendum, I don't think is right. It's a con."

DAVID CAMERON, APRIL 2010

"You think it is nasty? You ain't seen nothing yet... Tough shit."

.

DOMINIC CUMMINGS, VOTE LEAVE CAMPAIGN DIRECTOR, NOVEMBER 2015

"It is surely a boon for the world and for Europe that [Britain] should be intimately engaged with the EU. This is a market on our doorstep, ready for further exploitation by British firms: the membership fee seems rather small for all that access."

BORIS JOHNSON, FEBRUARY 2016

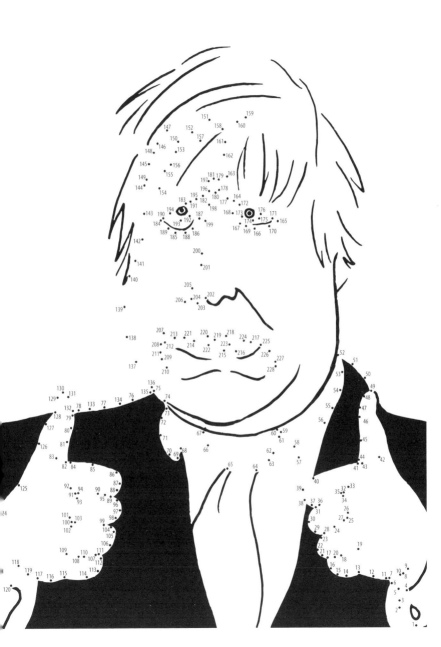

"There is only one way to get the change we need, and that is to vote to go…"

BORIS JOHNSON, FEBRUARY 2016

"I believe it is clearly
in our national interest to
remain a member of
the European Union."

THERESA MAY, APRIL 2016

"There must be no attempts
to remain inside the EU."

THERESA MAY, JUNE 2016

"In a 52–48 referendum, this would be unfinished business by a long way."

NIGEL FARAGE, MONTHS BEFORE HE DECLARED THAT SHOULD PRO-REMAINERS SUCCEED IN CALLS FOR A SECOND EU REFERENDUM, THEY WOULD BE BETRAYING "THE WISHES OF THE BIGGEST DEMOCRATIC EXERCISE IN THE HISTORY OF THIS NATION."

"Don't be taken in by
Project Fear."

BORIS JOHNSON, FEBRUARY 2016

PROJECT FEAR

EDITOR'S NOTE: THE AUTHOR INTENDED THAT THIS DOUBLE PAGE BE A SKETCH OF HEADLINES AND FRONT PAGES AND ARTICLES PUBLISHED BY SOME NEWSPAPERS.

THE ONES SUGGESTING WE WERE (OR TELLING US WE WERE) AWASH AND OVERRUN WITH MIGRANTS (MILLIONS OF THEM) WHO WERE GOING TO TAKE OUR JOBS AND OUR HOUSES AND SHOULD GO BACK TO WHERE THEY CAME FROM AND SHOULDN'T BE GRANTED ASYLUM BECAUSE THEY WERE ALL BOMBERS AND IF WE WEREN'T CAREFUL BRITAIN WOULD MERGE WITH FRANCE AND SLICED BREAD WOULD BE REPLACED WITH BAGUETTES.

YOU KNOW, THE REAL PROJECT FEAR.

HOWEVER, FOLLOWING LEGAL ADVICE, THE AUTHOR REALISED THAT TO DO THAT WITHOUT PERMISSION FROM THE NEWSPAPERS THAT CAME TO MIND MIGHT NOT BE A GOOD IDEA. BECAUSE PERMISSION MUST BE SOUGHT. AND OF COURSE SHOULD BE SOUGHT.

AND EVEN THOUGH THINGS LIKE "PERNICIOUS BULLSHITTERY" MAY HAVE COME TO THE AUTHOR'S MIND WHEN HE THOUGHT ABOUT SOME OF THE THINGS PRINTED IN MASSIVE BLACK LETTERS IN SOME NEWSPAPERS, IT OF COURSE ISN'T "PERNICIOUS BULLSHITTERY", IT IS JUST AN OPINION, AND TO COPY HEADLINES AND CAPTION THEM IN A WAY THAT SUGGESTED THEY WERE "PERNICIOUS BULLSHITTERY" COULD BE CONTSTRUED AS DEFAMATION. AND THINGS LIKE "I QUITE LIKE BAGUETTES" MAY ALSO HAVE COME TO MIND. ALL SORTS OF THINGS MAY HAVE COME TO MIND. LIKE "I HAVE A JOB." AND "NO MIGRANT HAS EVER TRIED TO STEAL MY JOB AS FAR AS I'M AWARE." THAT SORT OF THING. POSSIBLY.

SO INSTEAD, THE AUTHOR HAS DRAWN THREE THEN-EDITORS OF SOME NEWSPAPERS TO FILL THE SPACE AND ILLUSTRATE PROJECT FEAR AS BEST HE COULD. HE COULDN'T DRAW THE EDITORS FROM EVERY NEWSPAPER IN CIRCULATION BECAUSE THAT WOULD BE TOO MANY FACES TO PUT ON A SINGLE PAGE AND ALSO QUITE A LOT OF WORK. I IMAGINE.

Author's Note: we return to our regular programme on the following page. JW

"That's easy. When I go into Downing Street they do what I say; when I go to Brussels they take no notice."

RUPERT MURDOCH WHEN ASKED BY JOURNALIST ANTHONY HILTON WHY HE IS SO OPPOSED TO THE EU

The amount Vote Leave
told us the EU takes each
week that could be given to
the NHS instead.

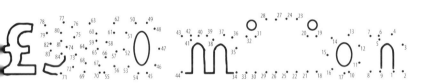

"The 350 million was an extrapolation [...] It was never the total."

IAIN DUNCAN SMITH, VOTE LEAVE, JUNE 2016

"People in this country have had enough of experts."

MICHAEL GOVE, JUNE 2016

% TRUST TO TELL THE TRUTH

NURSES: 94%

DOCTORS: 91%

TEACHERS: 87%

PROFESSORS: 85%

SCIENTISTS: 83%

JUDGES: 81%

WEATHER FORECASTERS: 76%

THE POLICE: 74%

TELEVISION NEWS READERS: 67%

CLERGY/PRIESTS: 65%

MAN/WOMAN IN THE STREET: 64%

CIVIL SERVANTS: 59%

VERACITY INDEX 2017:
ALL PROFESSIONS OVERVIEW

"Now I will read you a list of different types of people. For each would you tell me if you generally trust them to tell the truth or not?"

Base: 998 adults aged 15+, fieldwork 20-26 October 2017
IPSOS MORI, Social Research Institute

| 51 |
| 54 55 58 59 |
| 62 63 |
| 66 67 |
| 70 71 |
| 74 75 |
| 78 79 82 83 86 87 |
| 90 91 94 95 |

| 52 53 | 56 57 | 60 61 | 64 65 | 68 69 | 72 73 | 76 77 | 80 81 | 84 85 | 88 89 | 92 93 | 96 |

| LAWYERS: 54% | POLLSTERS: 50% | CHARITY CHIEF EXECUTIVES 50% | TRADE UNION OFFICIALS: 45% | LOCAL COUNCILLORS: 41% | BANKERS: 38% | BUSINESS LEADERS: 36% | EASTATE AGENTS: 27% | JOURNALISTS: 27% | PROFESSIONAL FOOTBALLERS: 26% | GOVERNMENT MINISTERS: 19% | POLITICIANS GENERALLY: 17% |

"We don't even have a British passport anymore!"

NIGEL FARAGE, JUNE 2016

EUROPEAN UNION
UNITED KINGDOM OF
GREAT BRITAIN
AND NORTHERN IRELAND

DIEU ET MON DROIT

SPORT

The will of the people.

23 JUNE 2016

VOTED REMAIN   **COULDN'T VOTE**

VOTED LEAVE   **DIDN'T VOTE**

"So much for the waning power of the print media."

TONY GALLAGHER, EDITOR-IN-CHIEF, THE SUN, LESS THAN AN HOUR
AFTER VICTORY FOR LEAVE WAS DECLARED, 23RD JUNE 2016

"We campaigned for Brexit. I don't think we caused Brexit."

TONY GALLAGHER, MAY 2017

"You're not laughing now are you?"

NIGEL FARAGE TO THE EUROPEAN PARLIAMENT, 28TH JUNE 2016

"Suck it up whiner."

STEWART JACKSON MP, NOW CHIEF OF STAFF AND SPECIAL ADVISOR TO DAVID DAVIS, IN RESPONSE TO BARRISTER AND WRITER RUPERT MYERS: "I CAN'T GET OVER THE FACT THAT THE WINNING SIDE LIED ABOUT A WHOLE BUNCH OF STUFF AND YET EXPECT US TO LIVE CHEERFULLY WITH THE RESULT."

"Common sense…suggests that the worst approach for the UK is to insist on the necessity of a 'deal' – we don't need one."

TIM MARTIN, FOUNDER AND CHAIRMAN OF WETHERSPOON, SEPTEMBER 2016

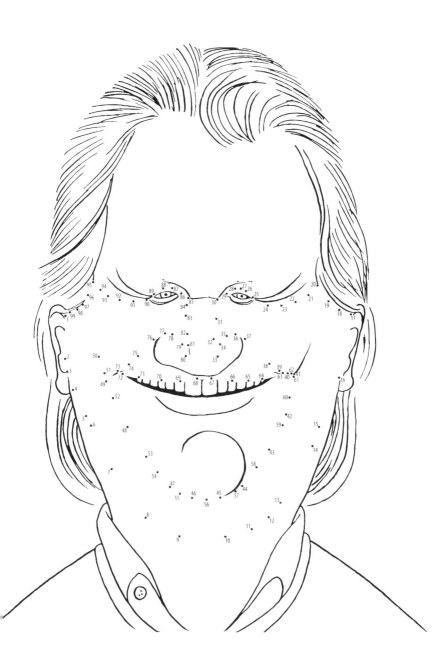

"If the man shot in Milan is the Berlin killer, then the Schengen Area is proven to be a risk to public safety. It must go."

NIGEL FARAGE, IN RESPONSE TO THE SHOOTING IN ITALY OF THE BERLIN TERRORIST ANIS AMRI

ANNUAL DEATHS FROM TERRORISM IN WESTERN EUROPE

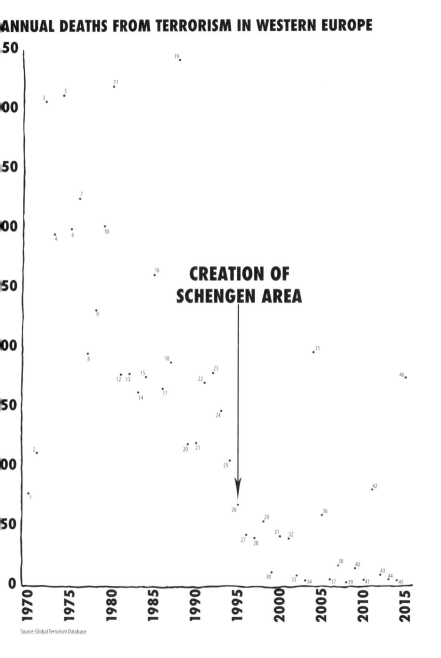

CREATION OF SCHENGEN AREA

Source: Global Terrorism Database

"You don't need a piece of paper with numbers on it to have an economic assessment."

DAVID DAVIS MP, SECRETARY OF STATE FOR EXITING THE EUROPEAN UNION, MARCH 2017

"I don't have to be very clever to do my job."

DAVID DAVIS

"It is a bit like the Gandhi thing – first they laugh at you, then they attack you, and then you win."

PAUL NUTTALL, UKIP LEADER, APRIL 2017

"Brexit was a war. We won."

AARON BANKS, MAJOR DONOR TO UKIP, APRIL 2017

"The free trade deal that we will have to do with the European Union should be one of the easiest in human history."

LIAM FOX, INTERNATIONAL TRADE SECRETARY, JULY 2017

"Henry VIII was a bastard, but he was my kind of bastard."

CONSERVATIVE MP EDWARD LEIGH IN PARLIAMENTARY DEBATE ON THE EU (WITHDRAWAL) BILL, SEPTEMBER 2017. THE BILL CONTAINS PROVISIONS KNOWN AS "HENRY VIII CLAUSES", WHICH GIVE GOVERNMENT THE ABILITY TO CREATE NEW POWERS FOR ITSELF WITHOUT RECOURSE TO PARLIAMENT

:'-(

TEXT MESSAGE FROM A SENIOR BRITISH AIDE TO POLITICO
AFTER THE DEMOCRATIC UNIONIST PARTY SCUPPERED A
BREXIT DEAL TO MOVE ON TO "PHASE 2"
OF NEGOTIATIONS WITH THE EU

"We hope to reach again a Europe united...a Europe in which men will be proud to say, 'I am a European.' We hope to see a Europe where men of every country will think as much of being a European as belonging to their native land, and that without losing any part of their love and loyalty to their birthplace. We hope that wherever they go in this wide domain, to which we set no limits in the European continent, they will truly feel, 'Here I am at home. I am a citizen of this country too.' "

WINSTON CHURCHILL, MAY 1948

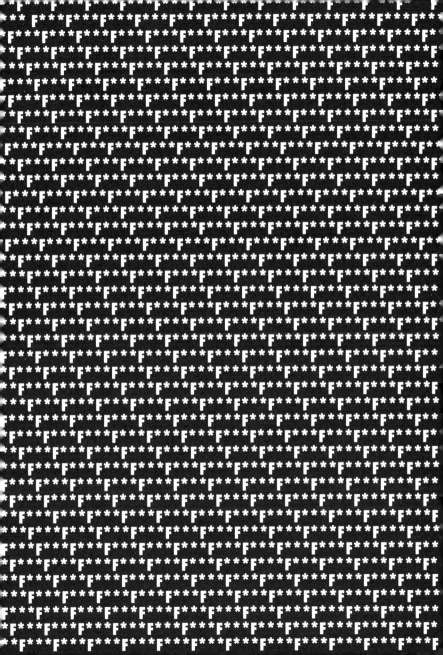